VASCO DA GAMA

Great Explorers
of the World

Discovering the Sea Route to India

Tony Napoli

Enslow Publishers, Inc.
40 Industrial Road
Box 398
Berkeley Heights, NJ 07922
USA
http://www.enslow.com

Library of Congress Cataloging-in-Publication Data

Napoli, Tony.
  Vasco da Gama : discovering the sea route to India / Tony Napoli.
      p. cm. — (Great explorers of the world)
  Includes bibliographical references and index.
  Summary: "Examines the life of explorer Vasco da Gama, including his childhood in Portugal, his three expeditions to India, opening up the spice trade and expanding Portugal's empire, and his legacy in world history"—Provided by publisher.
  ISBN-13: 978-1-59845-127-6
  ISBN-10: 1-59845-127-8
  1. Gama, Vasco da, 1469–1524—Juvenile literature. 2. Explorers—Portugal—Biography—Juvenile literature. 3. India—Discovery and exploration—Portuguese—Juvenile literature. 4. Africa—Discovery and exploration—Portuguese—Juvenile literature. 5. Discoveries in geography—Portuguese—Juvenile literature. I. Title.
  G286.G2N37 2010
  910.92—dc22
  [B]
                            2008046927

Printed in the United States of America

092009 Lake Book Manufacturing, Inc., Melrose Park, IL

10 9 8 7 6 5 4 3 2 1

To Our Readers: We have done our best to make sure all Internet Addresses in this book were active and appropriate when we went to press. However, the author and the publisher have no control over and assume no liability for the material available on those Internet sites or on other Web sites they may link to. Any comments or suggestions can be sent by e-mail to comments@enslow.com or to the address on the back cover.

♻ Enslow Publishers, Inc., is committed to printing our books on recycled paper. The paper in every book contains 10% to 30% post-consumer waste (PCW). The cover board on the outside of each book contains 100% PCW. Our goal is to do our part to help young people and the environment too!

Contents

Explorer Timeline

1469— Vasco da Gama is born in Sines, Portugal.

1492— Captures French vessels on the orders of King Dom João II.

1497— Chosen to command first Portuguese expedition to India.

— *July 8:* Fleet departs Lisbon for first voyage to India.

— *November 22:* Fleet rounds the Cape of Good Hope.

1498— *March:* Fleet lands at Mozambique Island and remains there for nearly a month.

— *May 20:* Fleet reaches Calicut on the Malabar coast of India.

— *August 29:* Fleet departs India for return trip to Portugal.

1499— *September:* Returns to Lisbon after first stopping in the Azores where his brother dies.

— *December 24:* Granted the title of Lordship of Sines.

1500–1501—Marries Dona Catarina de Ataíde.

1502— *February 10:* Main fleet of his second voyage to India leaves Lisbon.

— *September–October:* Captures and destroys a Muslim vessel, the *Mîrî*. Hundreds are killed.

— *November 1–3:* Heavily bombards Calicut.

1503— *February:* Wins decisive victory against large fleet of the Zamorin off Calicut.

— *February 20:* Fleet departs India for return trip to Portugal.

— *October 10:* Returns to Lisbon with large and valuable cargo of spices.

1507— He and his family are ordered to leave the town of Sines by King Dom Manuel.

1518— Petitions King Dom Manuel for title of Count.

1519— *December:* Granted title of Count of Vidigueira by King Dom Manuel.

1524— *January 26:* Named viceroy of India by King Dom João III.

— *April 9:* Fleet of third voyage to India departs Lisbon.

— *September:* Fleet reaches India, first stop at Chaul.

— *September–October:* Reaches Goa, then sails to Cochin. Begins major reforms of Portuguese India.

— *December 24:* Dies on Christmas Eve in Cochin.

Chapter 1

A Great Sea Voyage Ends in Glory

A thick haze settled on the water. Still, the men aboard the three ships could see mountains in the distance. Land—the first land they had seen in weeks. Captain-Major Vasco da Gama looked anxiously toward the shore. Could this be the destination he had been seeking for eleven months? Was it really India, gateway to the riches of the Far East? He was counting on his pilot, who knew this land, to tell him for certain.

The seas turned rough. The pilot had difficulty finding his way. Soon, he navigated closer to shore. He spoke to da Gama. "We have arrived," he said. "We are north of Calicut! Here is the land where you desired to go!"[1]

There is no record of what Vasco da Gama said when he heard this news. However, he must have been thrilled—and relieved. He and his men had traveled thousands of miles. They had braved many dangers and faced death several times. Now, on May 20, 1498, they had finally reached their goal. They had found an all-sea route from Europe to the land of India.

Vasco da Gama was from Portugal, a small country at the southwestern edge

Vasco da Gama landed on the shores of India in 1498 after traveling over rough seas for thousands of miles.

of Europe. He and more than 150 others had set sail from their homeland in July 1497. Their goal was to discover an all-sea route to India. No one from Europe had ever done that before. At that time, people in Europe did not know much about life in other faraway places of the world. Still, Europeans did know that India and the Far East held the possibility of great riches. The lands there offered valuable spices like pepper, as well as gold and diamonds. The country that opened a trade route could become very wealthy. A small country such as Portugal could become very powerful in a short time.

In some ways, that had already happened. Before Vasco da Gama ever reached India, Portugal had become a strong maritime, or seagoing, nation. This process began well before Vasco da Gama was born.

PORTUGAL BECOMES A MARITIME POWER

Portugal's rise as a strong seagoing nation began in the early 1400s. At the time, the country's ruler was King Dom João I (1385–1433). In 1415, he led an army across the waters to North Africa. This army then captured the town of Ceuta from the Moors. This allowed Portugal to gain a base from where it could explore the western coast of Africa. Soon, Portuguese traders brought back valuable

PRINCE HENRY
OF
PORTUGALL

Henry the Navigator helped make Portugal a very strong maritime power in the fifteenth century.

CEUTA

items to their country. These included gold, ivory, and slaves. The Portuguese were the first nation to use African slaves.

During this time, one man did much to make Portugal a strong maritime power—King Dom Joãos's third son, Henry. He became known as Prince Henry the Navigator. For more than forty years, Henry organized and paid for many sea voyages. Some of the best sailors, mapmakers, and shipbuilders went to work for him. During the mid-1400s, Henry's ships explored many islands in the North Atlantic Ocean. They traveled down the west coast of Africa, too. At the same time, many of these Portuguese travelers set up outposts or forts in several places.

Henry had more than one reason for wanting to explore these new places. Like most countries in Europe, Portugal was a Christian nation. For centuries, Christians and Muslims had battled to control lands. They also wanted to convert people to their religions. Henry was a leader of a religious and military group in his country called the Order of Christ. Many of the ships that Henry sent out had the cross of this Order on their sails.[2] The men who traveled on them had two goals. One was to bring back valuable goods to Portugal. The other was to convert anyone they met in new lands to the Christian faith.

During this time, Portugal explored and settled many new lands. It was the first country in Europe to settle many islands in the North Atlantic. These islands were Madeira, the Canaries, and the Azores. Portugal obtained many valuable resources from these places. Timber, wine, sugar, and very large amounts of grain were among the items shipped back to Portugal.

Henry died in 1460. By that time, Portugal had gained much from its sea voyages. The riches of Africa had been opened up. Still, Portugal was looking for new resources because competition from other nations was strong. By the time of Henry's death, the Portuguese had been forced to leave the Canaries. Within twenty years, Spain would control those islands.

The Portuguese knew that other riches, including valuable spices, could be found in the Far East.

But how could they get there by water? Many people believed it was possible to go around the bottom of Africa, and then sail across the Indian Ocean. It would take nearly another forty years to prove that. The person who eventually made the journey was born nine years after Henry died— Vasco da Gama.

Chapter 2

Early Life of an Explorer

Most historians believe that Vasco da Gama was born in Sines, Portugal,

in 1469.[1] In some places, his birth year is said to be 1460. There is a reason for this confusion. There are not many known facts about da Gama's early life. This is not unusual for someone born during that time. Not many documents or records were kept. Sometimes the ones that did exist got lost or destroyed.

Da Gama's family came from a region in Portugal called Alentejo. This area is in the southern part of Portugal. Da Gama's birthplace, Sines, is on the coast of the country. Many people who lived there made their living from the sea, trading goods or sailing on sea voyages.

Vasco da Gama did not come from a rich or noble family, but they were well known in their town. Da Gama's ancestors had helped Portugal's kings fight in wars. Da Gama's father, Estêvão, became a knight. For a time, he was the *alcaidemór*, or mayor, of Sines.[2] From this and other jobs he gained a certain amount of wealth and notoriety.

Estêvão da Gama married a woman named Dona Isabel Sodré, the daughter of

A statue of Vasco da Gama stands outside the Parish church of Sines, Portugal. Da Gama was born in his father's castle in Sines sometime in 1469.

DOM VASCO DA GAMA
1469 - 1524

DESCOBRIDOR E ALMIRANTE DO MAR DA INDIA
1º CONDE DA VIDIGUEIRA
VICE-REI DA INDIA

"...AQUELLE ILLUSTRE GAMA
QUE PARA SI DE INEAS TOMA A FAMA."
CAMÕES, LUS., I - 12

an important family. They had six sons and a daughter. Vasco spent his early years in his hometown near the ocean. Like other young boys there, he heard many tales of sea voyages. He learned about the many discoveries Portuguese explorers had made. These men had brought back riches to Portugal. They had fought battles against the Moors. Life at sea could be one great adventure after another. These stories probably excited young Vasco da Gama.

As a young man Vasco left home for a time. He traveled to a place called Évora, about seventy miles away. This city was larger than Sines. Many important people came there to do business. It was a very good place for a young man to get an education. At Évora, Vasco studied subjects that would be valuable to him as an explorer: math, navigation, and astronomy.

A HISTORIC VOYAGE

Before Vasco da Gama began his service to the Crown, King Dom João II had begun to think of sending a sea expedition to India. During the 1480s, Portuguese explorers had continued their voyages. They had made journeys down the west coast of Africa. The most important of these voyages was made in 1487 by Bartholmeu Dias. In August of that year, Dias set out from Portugal with three vessels. The ships traveled south along

In 1487, Bartholmeu Dias became the first European explorer to round the Cape of Good Hope—the southern tip of Africa.

the African coast. Weeks went by, and the weather turned stormy. Sometimes, the men lost sight of land for weeks, but they continued their journey.

Dias and his men made a few stops as they traveled south. Soon, the expedition reached the southern tip of the coast of Africa. No other European had ever gone that far before. The weather was so stormy that Dias and his men did not even realize what they had done.[3] They kept on sailing north, for nearly 500 miles. In early February 1488, the Portuguese saw mountains and entered what is known today as Mossel Bay. They finally realized they had been traveling *up* the East African coast. They had rounded the tip of Africa. This meant that the way to India, across the Indian Ocean, was now open for future voyages. There was great excitement aboard the ships.[4]

The vessels arrived back in Portugal in December 1488. Dias made a full report to King Dom João II. He gave the king a map showing the new region he had explored. Dias also gave a name to the southern tip of the African continent he had found. Remembering the miserable seas his crew had to fight, he called it the Cape of Storms. King Dom João II saw things differently. He believed the discovery would bring great riches to Portugal. He renamed the area the Cape of Good Hope.[5]

EARLY SERVICE TO THE CROWN

By 1492, Vasco da Gama, in his early twenties, performed his first service for the Portuguese Crown. King Dom João II was very angry with the French because they had captured a Portuguese ship filled with gold off the coast of Africa. The king wanted to take action against France. He ordered French vessels anchored in four Portuguese ports to be seized. He gave the job of taking the vessels in two of the ports to Vasco da Gama. A written account of the order is described by a historian of the time: "[King Dom João II] at once sent . . . Vasco da Gama . . . who was later to be Count of Vidigueira and Admiral of the Indies, a man whom he trusted and who had served in armadas and affairs of the sea, to do the same [capture] to those [ships] which might be there, which he did with great brevity."[6]

The mission was a great success. The French king, Charles VIII, soon released the Portuguese ship and its valuable cargo.

By 1495, Portugal had a new king. João II had died and his brother-in-law, Dom Manuel I, succeeded him. By this time, Vasco da Gama had gained more power. He had been given important titles by the royal family. One title was the Grand Master of the Order of Santiago, a very powerful religious order. With these titles came a rise in prestige and an increase in income.

PLANS FOR A VOYAGE TO INDIA

Vasco da Gama's rise in power and influence afforded him new opportunities. His life of exploration was ready to begin.

King Dom João II did not live to see a Portuguese explorer make the sea voyage to India. However, his successor, Dom Manuel, shared the former king's interest in the voyage. He felt it would bring honor and wealth to his country. So, he began to devote a great amount of time and effort to organizing an expedition to discover the all-sea route to Asia.

Finally in January 1497, the plans were in place. But the king had to choose the right person to lead the expedition. The success or failure of such a voyage would probably depend on who led it. Historians know the king chose Vasco da Gama. However, like many other details of Vasco da Gama's life, the reason he was chosen is not entirely clear.

Two Portuguese historians of the time claim that Vasco's father, Estêvão da Gama, was actually the first choice. He had been picked by King Dom João II two years earlier. By some accounts, Estêvão da Gama was the king's "most trusted navigator."[7] He was also thought to be an experienced captain.

Estêvão died before the expedition could ever be launched. Later, as a matter of family honor, King Dom Manuel chose his son Vasco. According to one story, the command was actually first offered to Vasco's older brother, Paulo, but he turned it down because of ill health.[8] This does not seem to make very much sense, though, because Paulo would make the trip to India as captain of one of the other vessels.

Many reasons went into King Dom Manuel's choice. Vasco da Gama had many qualities needed for the job. He was physically strong and familiar with the art of warfare. He had excellent maritime skills. He had a reputation of being hard, even ruthless, when needed. Yet he could also be diplomatic and understanding. All these qualities would be necessary for whoever commanded such a grand voyage. As its leader, he would meet the heads of many lands in Africa and then in India. He would be representing the king of Portugal, and his country. The job could only be trusted to someone ready for the responsibility.

Whatever the reasons for his selection, one thing is certain. Da Gama had been given a great honor. This would be Portugal's greatest sea expedition. Six months later, the building of the ships would be completed and the supplies gathered. Then Captain-Major Vasco da Gama set his course for the Far East and the riches of India.

FINAL PREPARATIONS

King Dom Manuel and his advisors decided to send four vessels on da Gama's voyage. The king chose another famous explorer to oversee the building of two of these ships—Bartholmeu Dias.

Dias had some new ideas. He remembered from his previous trip that his ships had been tossed about in the stormy seas at the Cape of Good Hope. Dias came up with a new kind of ship for da Gama's voyage.

Dias designed and built ships that were heavier and sturdier. The ships weighed about 100–120 tons and measured 75–85 feet long. Each had a flat bottom, with a high, square stern and bow. The cargo hold was divided into separate spaces. One contained room for firearms and other weapons. Another would hold water casks, extra cable, and riggings. The third would be for food and other supplies.

The ships also carried large weapons. Each ship had twenty heavy guns, made of wrought-iron. There were also a large number of crossbows, axes, spears, swords, and other hand weapons.[9]

The ships would also carry the most up-to-date maps and scientific equipment. Da Gama would have use of astronomical instruments, including astrolabes. He could also use tables with latitude readings, compasses, and an instrument that could help him determine high tides. Finally, the ships

Vasco da Gama took a fleet of four ships—*São Gabriel, São Rafael, Berrío,* and one unnamed supply ship—on his first voyage to India.

·S· Raphael·

·S· grauiel

❲ Vasquo da gama ❳

❲ Paullo da gama ❳

Jrmão de Vasco da gama á tornada pera Portugal, Varou e os bayxos Antre quilloa baça, aos quaes se chamão de S· Rafael por da Nao ... si se chamava, et a gente se Repartio pellas duas da companhia

borrio

❲ Nicolao coelho ❳

❲ goncallo nuñez ❳

Criado de Vasq da gama depois da Nao ter passado ho cabo de boa esperança et ser pouco avante da agoada de são bras se Repartirão os mantimentos et a gente della pellas outras da companhia, et depois de despe jada se poserá fogo /—

would carry large pillars of stone or marble. These exquisite pillars would bear a cross and the Portuguese Royal Arms. They were meant to be placed in various locations as the voyage continued. They would be landmarks to show the world proof of Portugal's success.[10]

The two large ships Bartholmeu Dias had designed were named the *São Gabriel* and the *São Rafael*. While the ships were being completed, Vasco da Gama was busy. He began to select and recruit his crews. Da Gama chose the *São Gabriel* as his flagship, which he would command. To command the *São Rafael*, da Gama chose his older brother, Paulo. The third ship in the fleet was the *Berrio*, a smaller and faster ship than the other two. Da Gama chose another experienced sailor as its captain. His name was Nicolau Coelho. The fourth ship on the voyage was an unnamed storeship. It would carry all the extra supplies needed. Its captain was Gonçalo Nunes, a man who had been one of da Gama's regular retainers.

There is no exact record of the total number of men who sailed with da Gama on his historic journey. Most historians put the number between 148 and 170. Each ship had many crewmembers. There would be a master (captain), a pilot, an assistant pilot, a mate, a boatswain, and many seamen.

In addition, the ships would carry condemned prisoners who would be given the chance to win a pardon. In exchange for their faithful service, they would be rewarded with their freedom—that is if they survived the journey. These men might be put ashore in certain dangerous places to check things out. They might also be left behind at an important port to help build goodwill for Portugal.[11]

Also on the voyage were three men who would fill very important roles. They were interpreters. These men would be valuable to the Portuguese in helping them communicate with African tribes, Arabs, and the people of India.

A FAREWELL CEREMONY

On July 8, 1497, the voyage began. The day before, da Gama and his officers had an audience with King Dom Manuel. They received permission to sail and instructions from the king. Da Gama also received letters from King Dom Manuel to give to leaders of the foreign lands the expedition would visit.

Later that day, da Gama and his men arrived in a town called Restelo. Their four ships were anchored nearby. The men were also there to attend church at Our Lady of Bethlehem (Belem), on the banks of the Tagus River. It had been built by Prince Henry the Navigator for seafarers. Vasco da Gama and his crewmembers kept an all-night

Vasco da Gama takes leave of King Dom Manuel at his departure from Lisbon, Portugal, for India on July 8, 1497.

vigil at the chapel. They prayed, confessed their sins, and asked for strength for their upcoming adventure. The next morning they led a march down to the water. They were followed by priests saying prayers. A great many people lined the route as the men walked on.

When they reached the water's edge, they knelt down in silence. The priests offered up forgiveness for anyone who might die on the journey. Then da Gama and his men rowed out to their ships. The king's royal standard was set above the *São Gabriel*. The sails with the great red cross of the Order of Christ were unfurled. The four ships set off down the river.[12]

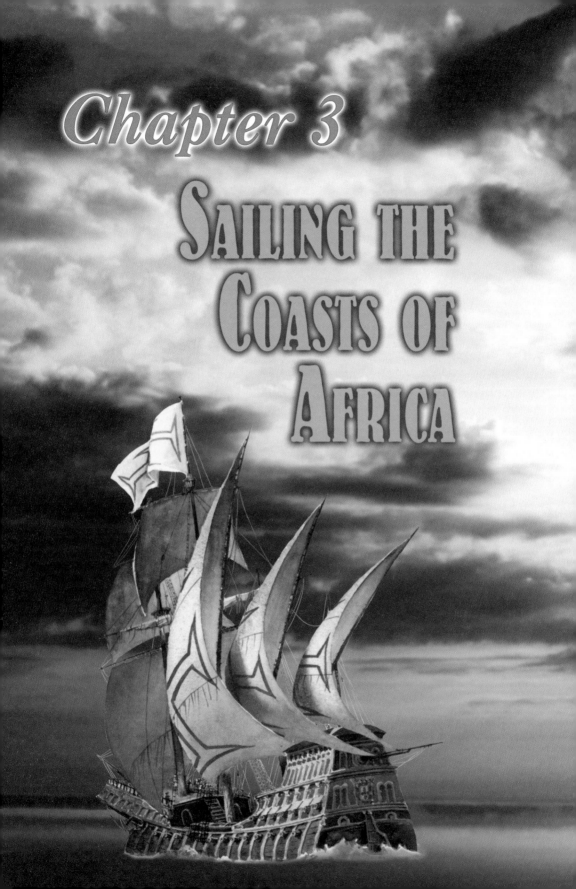

Chapter 3

SAILING THE COASTS OF AFRICA

Much of what historians know today about da Gama's great journey comes from a single source: a journal-logbook called the *Roteiro*. It was written by one of the crewmembers on the *São Rafael*. The journal was discovered in the mid-1830s in a Portuguese monastery. The author of the journal is unknown. Many historians have tried for centuries without success to learn his identity.

While the author of the journal has remained unknown, no one doubts that it is authentic. It has been very useful for historians who needed an eyewitness account of the da Gama voyage. Before the journal was discovered, Portuguese historians had written the only details of the journey decades after it took place. The *Roteiro* remains a wonderful source for a first-hand description of what happened during those many months of the da Gama expedition.

THE FIRST MONTHS AT SEA

The early days of the journey went smoothly. In addition to da Gama's four ships, one other vessel had come along. It was a ship carrying men and supplies to a place called São Jorge de Mina, along the west coast of Africa (near present-day Ghana). Portugal had built a fort there after an earlier expedition. The captain of this other ship, Bartholmeu Dias, took over the fort's command.

A week after leaving Portugal, the ships sighted the Canary Islands. Then they set a more easterly course, to come close to the African coast. In mid-July, the ships encountered a thick fog, common to that coastline. Soon, they lost sight of one another. Da Gama knew something like this could happen. If it did, he had instructed all the ships to sail for the Cape Verde Islands where they would be able to reunite.

All went according to the plan. On July 27, the entire fleet dropped anchor at Santiago. This was the largest of the Cape Verde Islands. The ships were inspected and fresh supplies of water, meat, and wood were put onboard. On August 3, all the ships left Santiago harbor.

At this point, Dias's ship left the fleet for São Jorge de Mina. Da Gama took his ships on his own course. Two weeks later, the main mast of the *São Gabriel* broke in a storm. It took two days to fix. Soon, da Gama ordered his fleet to sail south and west, in a circular motion, away from the African coast. It was a very unusual move.

Da Gama chose this different route because he had learned something from earlier Portuguese explorers. He knew that sailing away from the African coast would be a quicker way of reaching the Cape of Good Hope. His fleet would avoid the stormy weather and coastal winds that had slowed earlier voyages and damaged ships. This route would eventually take his ships very close to South America. They would come within 660 miles of the coast of what is today the country of Brazil.

Weeks, and then months, went by. When the ships sailed below the area known as the Tropic of Capricorn, they headed southeast. The weather turned colder, the seas rougher. The winds picked up, and that allowed the ships to make good time. By then the ships were beginning to smell. Nearly all the fresh food was gone, and the fresh water had gone bad. But if the crew was worried, there was no sign of it. Da Gama seemed to have the confidence of his men.

Finally, on October 27, they saw whales and seals, and coastal seaweed. This was a good sign. It meant they were nearing land. On November 4, at 9:00 A.M., they sighted land. The ships came together and the crews shouted with joy and relief. The banners and standards were raised and the ships fired their guns to celebrate.[1] The vessels moved closer to shore. However, da Gama and his officers were not certain where they were.

The ships continued farther south. Three days later the fleet came upon a wide bay. The ships

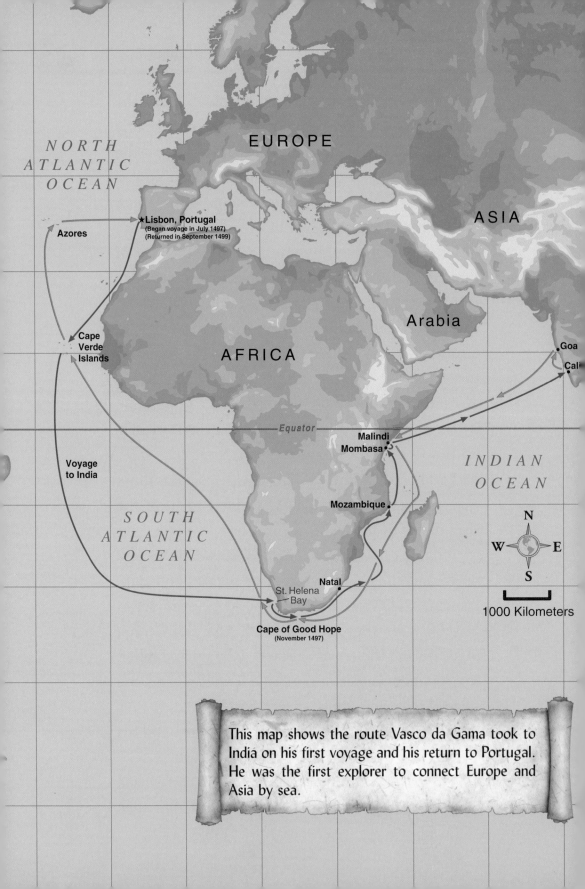

NORTH
ATLANTIC
OCEAN

EUROPE

ASIA

★Lisbon, Portugal
(Began voyage in July 1497)
(Returned in September 1499)

Azores

Arabia

Cape
Verde
Islands

AFRICA

Goa
Cal

Equator

Malindi
Mombasa

INDIAN
OCEAN

Voyage
to India

SOUTH
ATLANTIC
OCEAN

Mozambique

N
W E
S

Natal

1000 Kilometers

St. Helena
Bay

Cape of Good Hope
(November 1497)

This map shows the route Vasco da Gama took to
India on his first voyage and his return to Portugal.
He was the first explorer to connect Europe and
Asia by sea.

anchored there. Da Gama named it St. Helena Bay. This part of the voyage had taken more than three months. They had sailed more than 3,300 miles without using one landmark to help them find their way. Still, da Gama knew the hardest part of the journey was yet to come. They still had to go around the Cape of Good Hope and sail up the east coast of Africa. Then they had to find their way to India.

A BRIEF STAY

Da Gama went ashore to get a good idea of where they had landed. He determined that they were about one hundred miles north of the Cape of Good Hope. Da Gama ordered the ships to be cleaned thoroughly. Whatever repairs that were needed would also be done. The ships would take on wood and fresh water. A nearby source was found for fresh water and da Gama named it the Santiago River.

During their stay, the Portuguese came into contact with the local people. Over the next few days, nearly fifty tribesmen appeared. They accepted gifts from da Gama's men, who in turn received souvenirs from the natives. These friendly relations went on for several days. Then a misunderstanding between one of da Gama's men, Fernão Velloso, and the natives led to violence.

Velloso had gone with some local people to their village. They had hunted seal and then cooked it. Then the natives had become angry, and ordered Velloso to return to his ship. Before long, Velloso was seen running toward the ships while the natives ran after him. Several of da Gama's men were hunting whales at the time and the entire scene became one of confusion.

Da Gama ordered all rowboats back to the ships while Velloso ran to jump aboard. Just then, the natives began throwing stones and shooting arrows. One of the arrows hit da Gama in the leg. The wound was not serious. As the Portuguese moved offshore, the natives could be seen yelling in anger.

Da Gama later ordered some of his own men ashore fully armed with arrows to take action against the natives. He felt he could not sail away letting them believe the Portuguese were weak and helpless. There is no record of how many people were wounded or killed, if any, in this affair. The author of the *Roteiro* noted the reaction of the crew to the event. "All this happened because we looked upon these people as men of little spirit, quite incapable of violence, and had therefore landed without first arming ourselves."[2] It was something da Gama and his crew would not let happen again.

ROUNDING THE CAPE

Da Gama's fleet remained at St. Helena Bay for eight days. They sailed away on November 16, and two days later they sighted the Cape of Good Hope. However, the winds were very strong and the seas turned rough. This prevented the ships from rounding the Cape. For four days da Gama's ships battled the strong winds and sea. Finally, at noon on November 22, the fleet "doubled," or rounded, the Cape. There was great relief and joy on board. On the 25th, they sailed into the Bay of São Bras and dropped anchor. Today it is known as Mossel Bay.

The fleet remained there for thirteen days. The ships took on fresh water and more wood. Da Gama also ordered that the storeship be broken apart and its supplies given to the other three vessels. As they did at St. Helena Bay, the Portuguese had contact with the local people.

The first contact went well. Da Gama's men exchanged some trinkets with a small group of locals who greeted them. Then two days later, a much larger group of natives came up to the ships. Nearly two hundred men, driving cattle and sheep, warmly greeted the newcomers. Soon, a feast with dancing and music was held. Things were going so well that even the captain-major himself began to dance.[3]

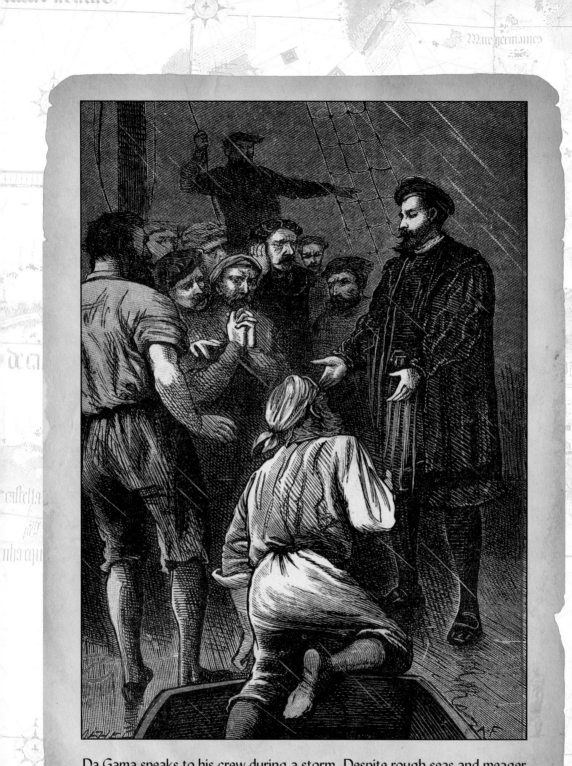

Da Gama speaks to his crew during a storm. Despite rough seas and meager supplies, da Gama and his crew rounded the Cape of Good Hope.

However, the next day relations turned bad. A dispute came up over a Portuguese crewmember's wish to take water from a certain source. The locals objected and then refused to make another exchange of goods. Da Gama remembered what happened at St. Helena Bay. He told his men to wear their armor and arm themselves. Then he ordered two shots fired from one of his ships. The shots caused a panic among the locals. They fled up into the hills.

The fleet left São Bras on December 7. Before they did, they left behind two objects to mark their landing there. One object was a pillar, or *padrão*, they had brought with them from Portugal. The other object was a large wooden cross made from the broken storeship. Their earlier actions had made the natives angry. The author of the *Roteiro* describes what happened as they were leaving. "When about to set sail, we saw about ten or twelve negroes, who demolished both the cross and the pillar before we had left."[4] This would not be the last time that some local peoples would show their anger as the Portuguese departed their shores.

TRAVELING ALONG AFRICA'S EAST COAST

Vasco da Gama's fleet began to sail farther up the East African coast. Progress was slow and difficult.

On December 16, the ships passed the farthest point of the Dias expedition. On December 25, da Gama named the land they were slowly passing by Natal. It was the Portuguese word for Christmas. Drinking water was soon in short supply again, and they had to find a port. On January 11, 1498, the fleet dropped anchor at the mouth of a small river in southern Mozambique.

The Portuguese were greeted in a friendly manner by the African people. Two translators went ashore and were well-received. Da Gama sent gifts to the local chief and the Portuguese were told they were welcome to take whatever supplies they needed. The fleet took on much needed wood and water, and after five days set sail again.

By January 25, the fleet had reached the mouth of the Quelimane River. This river is a tributary of the Zambezi. The local people in this land were very similar in language and custom to the land da Gama's fleet had just left. The men and women wore only loincloths because of the high humidity and heat. The land was filled with marshes and many large trees. There was also a great deal of fruit which the locals ate in great amounts.

In fact, the Africans offered fruit and other food to da Gama's men as gifts. The fleet stayed there for a month. They repaired a mast on the *São Rafael* and took on water. Many of the men became ill with scurvy, a serious disease caused by a lack of vitamin C. Their hands and feet swelled. Their gums grew over their teeth, which became loose, so they could not eat. Da Gama's brother, Paulo, helped tend to the sick. He shared his own personal supply of medicine with the crew. He looked after them, visiting the sick each day.[5] The men widely praised him for doing this and they soon became well.

On February 24, the fleet continued on its long voyage. A week later, they had traveled northeast about three hundred miles. They were heading through the Mozambique Channel, between Africa and Madagascar. On March 2, the crew sighted Mozambique Island and anchored their ships. Soon, local people in canoes came out to meet them. They offered to show da Gama's fleet the way into port.

Da Gama could tell from their appearance that these natives were "Moors." (The Portuguese used the term Moors to describe all Muslims they met.) In fact, da Gama's fleet had reached a part of Africa where nearly all of the native tribes were Muslim. For many centuries the Islamic faith had been strong in this region.

Soon, da Gama had a meeting with the local ruler, or sultan. The sultan visited two of the ships and had dinner with da Gama. Then the sultan entertained the Portuguese in his home. At first these visits were friendly, and gifts were exchanged. Da Gama gave the sultan a red hood, food, hats, corals, and other items. However, the sultan was not impressed with these things. He asked for a gift of scarlet cloth. When he was told the Portuguese had none to offer, he became upset.

Da Gama knew he was going to need help during this last part of the voyage. He wanted to have people onboard who knew these unfamiliar waters. He asked the sultan to provide him with two pilots for the rest of the trip. The sultan said yes. Da Gama agreed to pay them on one condition. One of the pilots always had to remain onboard if the other wanted to go ashore.

Soon, relations between the Portuguese and the Muslims became tense. On March 10, da Gama moved his ships well out into the bay. When one of the pilots escaped, da Gama sent men to capture him. As they rowed toward shore, they were attacked by Muslim archers in boats. One of the Portuguese ships fired guns, and the Muslims retreated.

On March 11, da Gama's fleet sailed off. Bad winds stopped them, and four days later, they were back where they had started. During the next two weeks, da Gama tried to take on much needed fresh water for his ships, but the sultan would not allow it. The two sides came to open warfare over the issue. The Portuguese used their artillery to bombard the Muslims and the town.

Finally, the ships took on the needed water without any more trouble. On March 29, the fleet left Mozambique Island. They took several captured Muslims with them. They traveled north along the coast, and on April 7, the fleet reached the port of Mombasa.

An Arab ship filled with armed men came out to meet them. Da Gama would only let a few of them board his ship. The following day, the local sultan sent a few men to represent him. They carried gifts and said they were Christians. They told da Gama he could enter the port without fear and take what supplies he needed. Da Gama sent two of his own men into town and the sultan received them. Later they reported back what they had seen. The two men "saw many prisoners walking about . . . in irons . . . and these, it seemed to us, must have been Christians, because the Christians in this land are at war with the Moors."[6]

On April 10, the fleet dropped anchor outside the harbor. Da Gama was still suspicious. That afternoon Muslim vessels had surrounded his ships with many men. That night, he asked two of the captured Muslims from Mozambique Island to tell him what the local sultan was up to. They said they knew nothing. So da Gama had the men tortured with drops of boiling oil. The men then

confessed that the sultan was planning to attack and capture da Gama's fleet. It would be revenge for what had happened in Mozambique.

At midnight the attack began. Some Muslims entered the water and began to climb aboard the ships to damage them. They were discovered and the Portuguese sounded an alarm. The attackers then fled. The author of the *Roteiro* says, "our Lord did not allow them to succeed because they were unbelievers."[7]

Da Gama wanted to remain at Mombasa. The warm climate helped his crew regain their health, but he knew it was too dangerous to stay. The next attack might succeed. So on April 13, they set sail again.

A FINAL STOP AND A FRIENDLY PORT

The next day, the fleet came upon two boats. They gave chase in order to capture them. The purpose was to find a good pilot. They captured one of the boats, which was filled with gold, silver, and other goods. They also captured a young woman and her husband, an old Moor.

On April 14, they dropped anchor off the port of Malindi. The next day, da Gama sent the man he had captured to visit the local sultan. He told him to tell the ruler he had come in peace. Later, the sultan sent a messenger to da Gama with gifts.

He also told the captain-major the sultan said he would give the Portuguese the supplies they needed. And he would let him have the pilot he wanted so badly.

A few more days went by, but no pilot appeared. When the sultan sent a servant out to represent him, da Gama took him hostage. He sent word to the sultan that he would release the hostage if he got the pilot he had been promised. The ruler then sent a pilot on board, and the servant was let go.

The crew was said to be "much pleased" with this man, whom they believed to be a Christian.[8] However, it is not certain whether the man was a Christian, Hindu, or Muslim. Historians cannot agree on his identity. But they do know he was well-trained and experienced. The new pilot had made the trip from East Africa to western India many times.

Da Gama finally had the last important thing he had been missing. After nine days, the fleet left Malindi. They had been away from home for nine months. They had traveled thousands of miles, battling bad weather and serious illness. They had faced angry local peoples. But through it all, they had survived. Da Gama was ready to take the final step to India.

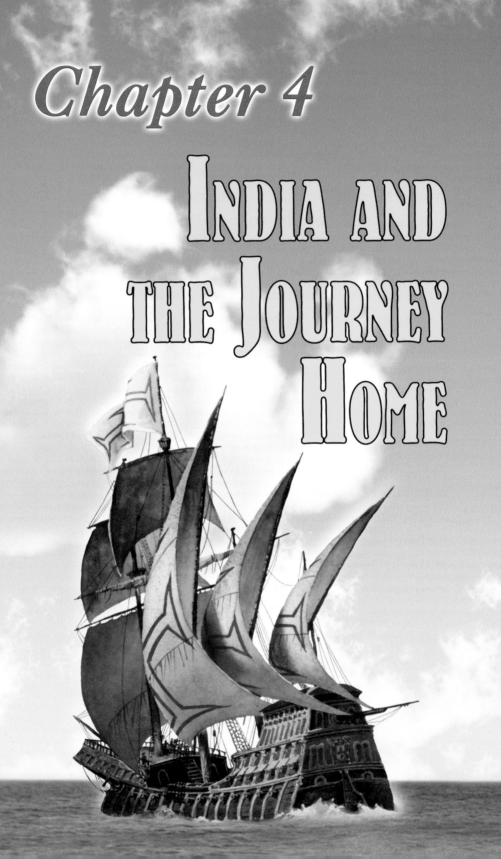

Chapter 4

India and the Journey Home

The trip across the Arabian Sea to India took twenty-three days. Luckily, the voyage was fairly smooth. Da Gama and his men sighted land and mountains on May 18, 1498. Bad weather forced them to stay offshore for two days. Finally, on May 20, the fleet anchored just north of Calicut, on India's Malabar Coast.

The Malabar Coast is more than five hundred miles long. At this time, it was made up of several small states, or kingdoms. Often, these states did not get along with one another. They fought over control of the rich spice trade in the region. The most valuable of these spices was pepper.

The most important of the Indian states was Calicut. It had the best pepper production. It was also a place where many trade routes came together. These routes connected East Africa, India, Persia, China, and other places.

People of the Hindu faith governed Calicut. They called their ruler *Samduri raja*, meaning "King of the Sea." The Portuguese called him the Zamorin.[1] Hindus made up much of the population of

This Flemish tapestry depicts Vasco da Gama's fleet arriving at Calicut in 1498.

Calicut. But people of all faiths and nationalities lived and worked there.

Calicut was a great center for trade. Its markets were filled with people who had come from Persia, China, Syria, Turkey, and other foreign lands. Christians and Jews both lived and traded there. However, the most powerful group was the

Muslims. There were two main groups. One group was made up of foreign Arab traders who lived in the city. The other group was from the area, called Kerala Muslims, or *Mappilas*.

The religion of Islam had spread to India many years before. The Muslims there had become powerful by showing favor to the Zamorin. They had given him many gifts. As a result, they had their own shops and warehouses in one part of the city. They had many ships, as well. They were wealthy and controlled much of Calicut's trade. The Portuguese soon found out that this was not good news. The Muslims did not want Christians to come to Calicut and take away any of their trade. They would do everything they could to prevent that.

THE FIRST MEETING WITH THE ZAMORIN

Four small boats filled with men greeted da Gama's fleet. The men spoke Arabic, so da Gama sent one of his own men, João Nunes, into town with them. Nunes was brought to meet two Arabs from Tunis who spoke Spanish. These two men said to Nunes, "What the Devil? What brought you hither?" Nunes replied, "We came in search of Christians and spices."[2]

One of the Arabs returned with Nunes to the ships. The Arab told da Gama that the ruling Zamorin was not in Calicut. He was in the town of Ponnani, about twenty-eight miles south. Da Gama sent word there that a representative of the king of Portugal had come bearing letters of introduction. The Zamorin sent word back that he would return to Calicut to meet with him.

Da Gama's meeting with the Zamorin took place on May 28, 1498. Da Gama went ashore with thirteen of his men. One of these men was the author of the *Roteiro*.

Da Gama and his men dressed in their finest clothes. When they reached Calicut, six of da Gama's men carried him through the city in a *palanquin*, or covered litter. Hundreds of people lined the streets to see the visitors. The author of the *Roteiro* described these people as having light brown faces. Many people had beards and long hair. Others had their hair cut short or had shaved heads. The women "wear many jewels of gold round the neck, [and] numerous bracelets on their arms. . . . All these people are well-dressed and apparently of mild temper." Despite their dress and appearance, the *Roteiro*'s author believed that Calicut was "inhabited by Christians."[3]

The Zamorin received da Gama and his men in a courtyard. Signs of the ruler's great wealth surrounded him. He sat on a couch covered in green velvet. By his side were bowls and basins made of gold. Using an interpreter, the Zamorin asked da Gama why he had come to India. Through his interpreter, da Gama told him that he came representing the king of Portugal. He said this king was "the Lord of many countries" and possessed great wealth. He told the Zamorin that they had traveled far to seek out the Christians they knew lived in many places in both Africa and India. Of course,

Vasco da Gama (standing center) delivers King Dom Manuel's letter to the Zamorin (seated left), ruler of the Hindu people in Calicut, India.

da Gama said, the Portuguese also came to India to join in the trade for spices.

Da Gama also said that King Dom Manuel was eager to enter into a "friendship" with such a powerful leader as the Zamorin. He asked the ruler to let him take ambassadors from India back home to Portugal. The Zamorin said the Portuguese were welcome. He also agreed to send his representatives to Portugal.

THE MUSLIMS CAUSE PROBLEMS

Da Gama and his men spent the night in town in a house prepared for them. The day had gone well for them. Da Gama hoped for good relations with the Zamorin. However, the relationship began to sour the next day.

Da Gama brought several items from Portugal as gifts to give the Zamorin. He had cloth, strings of coral, hand basins, a case of sugar, and casks of oil and honey. When da Gama showed these gifts to the Zamorin's assistant and Arab merchants, the men laughed. They said these gifts were not good enough to present to such a high ruler. Any average merchant or trader would give these gifts. The only proper gift was gold.

Da Gama explained that these gifts were from him, an ambassador, not his king. One day he would return bearing gold from King Dom Manuel as a gift. The assistant refused to let him take these gifts to the Zamorin. Da Gama insisted he still needed to meet with the ruler again. Although the men promised they would return later and take him, they did not.

This episode began many weeks of problems for the visitors. The next day, da Gama had another meeting with the Zamorin. It did not go well. The Zamorin was not pleased when he heard about the gifts da Gama had brought. He demanded to see the formal letter the captain-major had brought from King Dom Manuel. The two men then discussed what trade products could be found in Portugal. The Zamorin told da Gama to anchor his ships and unload his cargo. He could then sell it for the best offers he received.

The Portuguese would soon find out that there were powerful people working against them. These people were the Muslim traders and merchants who had been in Calicut for years. They held great influence with the Zamorin and his royal court. These Muslims did not want to see the

Portuguese Christians gain access to India's rich spice trade.

Da Gama and his men returned to their ships on June 2. The Portuguese unloaded some of their goods for sale in town. However, many of the Muslim merchants spread the word that the goods were of poor quality. Through all of June, July, and into August, the Portuguese sold little of their merchandise. However, da Gama let many of his crew members take turns going ashore. This allowed them to trade for local goods as they wished. These men were treated well by the local Hindus. They even received food and shelter in many places.

In turn, da Gama welcomed local Hindus who came out to his ships to trade. The Portuguese exchanged such items as bracelets, clothes, and other articles. In return, they got samples of items to bring back home. These included spices, such as cloves, cinnamon, and pepper, and also valuable stones. In this way, da Gama also learned much about the rich Indian spice trade. He learned where the spices came from and how long it took for them to reach Calicut. He also learned how they were shipped to other lands and how they were priced. This was very valuable information to take home to Portugal.[4]

PREPARING TO LEAVE

By early August, da Gama believed it was time to prepare for the trip home. Still he had more problems. Da Gama sent one of his men, Diego Dias, to the Zamorin. Dias brought with him gifts and a message telling the ruler of da Gama's wish to leave Calicut. The Zamorin held Dias hostage and demanded a payment of "duties" before letting the Portuguese sail away.

Soon, da Gama took some hostages of his own. He sent word to the Zamorin that he would kill them unless Dias and some other Portuguese men were released. Several days later, the Zamorin gave in. Dias and the other men were let go. Da Gama let some of his hostages go, too. However, he reached an agreement with the Zamorin to take some natives back with him to Portugal. He wanted living proof to show King Dom Manuel that he had indeed reached India.

The Zamorin also sent back a letter to King Dom Manuel. In it he wrote that "Vasco da Gama, a gentleman of your household, came to my country, whereat I was pleased. My country is rich in cinnamon, cloves, ginger, pepper, and precious stones. That which I ask of you in exchange is gold, silver, corals, and scarlet cloth."[5]

On August 29, 1498, the fleet pulled up anchor, hoisted their flags, and fired their cannons. After three months in India, they headed for home.

Vasco da Gama had to fend off many enemies at sea during his first voyage to India.

BATTLES AT SEA

The voyage home turned out to be difficult. The fleet would have to fight against bad weather and severe illness. They would also have to fight off enemies.

On August 30, the fleet was only a few miles away from Calicut. The winds were calm. As they waited for the winds to pick up, they saw about seventy boats with armed men approach. Da Gama knew these were hostile ships. When they were close enough, he ordered his ships to fire upon them. The winds picked up and the Portuguese fleet sailed off. The armed boats followed until a thunderstorm hit. The storm allowed da Gama's fleet to rapidly sail away. The smaller ships were forced to break off their pursuit.[6]

On September 20, the fleet anchored at the Anjedive Islands, south of Goa. They stayed for nearly two weeks. Here the ships were cleaned. The fleet also took on more wood, water, and vegetables. Over the next several days, the Portuguese fleet had to fight off more hostile ships. They fired upon eight vessels, which they later learned had come from Calicut to capture or kill them. Two days later, they fought off another surprise assault by two large ships. Da Gama later found out these were pirate ships that wanted to seize the Portuguese fleet.

On October 5, 1498, da Gama's fleet began the trip back across the Arabian Sea. The journey took more than three months. Often, there were no strong winds to carry the ships along. At other times, the winds blew in the wrong direction. Progress was very slow. They ran out of fresh fruits and vegetables and the water went bad. Worse, many men came down with scurvy again. On the journey to India, some thirty men had died of the disease. On the trip home, another thirty men died. By December, only seven or eight men on each ship were able to work.

Finally, on January 2, 1499, they sighted land once again. Five days later, the fleet anchored off the port of Malindi. On the trip to India, this had been the friendliest place they had visited. Now, da Gama hoped once again to be treated well. He needed to repair his ships and take on food and water. Luckily, the local sultan gave them oranges, fowl, eggs, and other supplies. Da Gama sent a present to the sultan and asked for a tusk of ivory in return to take to King Dom Manuel. He also asked that a *padrão* be built as a sign of friendship. The sultan agreed.

On January 11, the fleet left Malindi. Two days later, at another stop, da Gama decided to combine his fleet into two ships. There were not enough healthy crewmembers to man all three ships. They took everything of value off the *São*

Rafael and placed it on the *São Gabriel* and the *Berrio*. Then they burned the *São Rafael*. The two ships then continued their trip south.

The fleet rounded the Cape of Good Hope on March 20, 1499. The men were thrilled to have made it back around this landmark. They knew they were now on the final leg of their journey.

TRAGEDY AND A JOYFUL HOMECOMING

The fleet had nearly a month of good weather and strong winds. They reached the Cape Verde Islands by April 16. They were near the Guinea coast by April 25. At this point, the events described in the *Roteiro* come to an end. Historians do not know why. Some believe the author may have gotten off the ship and stayed in Africa. Still, historians do know what happened during the final weeks of the voyage.

In late April, the *São Gabriel* and the *Berrio* got separated in a storm. Nicolau Coelho took his ship as quickly as possible back home to Portugal. The *Berrio* arrived outside Lisbon on July 10, 1499. It had been at sea for 732 days.

Da Gama took the *São Gabriel* to the island of Santiago. There, he turned command of the ship over to João de Sá, one of his officers. He told de Sá to sail for Lisbon as soon as possible. Although he was eager to get home, too, da Gama had another serious thing to worry about. His brother Paulo was very ill. He wanted to return to Portugal to get him the best medical care. At the least, he did not want to have to bury him at sea.

Da Gama arranged to get a faster, smaller vessel and headed for Lisbon. Paulo's condition got worse. Da Gama stopped on the island of Teixeira in the Azores. There, his brother died. Da Gama had him buried with full honors. Then he sadly headed for home.

After the *Berrio* had arrived in July 1499, word had quickly spread of the fleet's successful voyage to India. Celebrations and feasts were held. King Dom Manuel was pleased, but he was anxious for the leader of the voyage to return home. He wanted to hear all about the adventure from Vasco da Gama.

The *São Gabriel* returned to Lisbon sometime in August. Da Gama arrived sometime between August 29 and September 14, 1499. The exact dates are not known.

Word quickly spread throughout Lisbon of da Gama's return. People were greatly excited by the news. Church bells rang. Celebrations were held in many places. A royal welcome from King Dom Manuel awaited him.

Chapter 5

A Hero to His Country

Even before his return, Vasco da Gama had become famous in his country. The surviving crewmembers from the *Berrio* had been describing their two-year voyage since their return in July. They told of the difficult weather they had fought. They described the hostile peoples they met in many places in Africa. They told of the problems they had in India, especially with the powerful Muslims in Calicut.

In all these stories, the men said that they only survived to return home because of Vasco da Gama. They described da Gama's courage and skill in navigating the stormy seas, and told of his bravery in attacking the Muslims who wanted to capture or kill the Portuguese. All these men gave credit to da Gama for the voyage's success. Without him, many said, the men might have been put in irons in a foreign land or even killed.

These stories had spread during the weeks before da Gama's arrival. Now, people cheered him as he walked down the street. Only thirty years old, he had become a hero to his country.

The king held a royal ceremony for da Gama and his officers. The captain-major presented the king with gifts from India. These gifts included gems, necklaces, and valuable Chinese porcelain. In turn, Dom Manuel had gifts for the members of the crew. He presented clothes from his wardrobe to the seamen. And he gave royal horses to the officers. He also made good on a promise he had made before the voyage began. He gave money to the widows and orphans of crewmembers who had died on the journey.[1] As for Vasco da Gama, his rewards, both in money and power, would soon come.

A HISTORIC VOYAGE BRINGS CHANGE TO PORTUGAL

Da Gama's successful voyage to India would have a great effect on his country and the rest of Europe. Of course, the trip did not come without a cost. Many men lost their lives. Again, no records exist with the exact number. Some estimates claim that about half the crew, which numbered between 150 and 175 men, was lost.[2] Some historians believe only forty to fifty men survived the voyage.[3] Many of them who returned had serious health problems. Still, Portugal gained many benefits from da Gama's journey.

The fleet had traveled some 23,000 nautical miles. It was the first voyage in history connecting the West and East by sea. The ships brought back many spices, such as cinnamon, cloves, and pepper. They had also brought back valuable gems. Da Gama returned with something even more important. He came back with great knowledge about India.

King Dom Manuel was quick to let other countries know of the success of the voyage. He wrote letters to important people in Europe. He wrote to Spain's King Ferdinand and Queen Isabella. He also wrote to Pope Alexander VI. In these letters he described what da Gama's voyage had discovered. He had found "large cities, large edifices, and rivers, and great populations, among whom is carried on all the trade in spices and precious stones." The letter went on to say that da Gama had also found many Christians in India. These Christians were "not yet strong in the faith or possessed of a thorough knowledge of it." However, the king wrote, once they were "fortified in the faith, there will be an opportunity for destroying the Moors of those parts."[4]

King Dom Manuel took other steps to honor the historic achievement. He ordered that a new gold coin be struck to commemorate the voyage. He also began a new public works program. The king believed the Portuguese would now be a strong force in the spice trade. He had new royal dockyards and warehouses built.

Terra del Rey de portugall

Mare oceanus

Os montes claros em affrica

Serra lioa   Castello damina

Mare occeanus:

This map of Africa and Europe was made in 1502 after da Gama returned from his voyage to India.

Ceuus aticus:

ieruladem:

 caeri:

is:

Mare barbaricus:

Oceanus yndicus meridionalis.

Circulus capricorni:

Mare prasod

REWARDS AND ACCLAIM FOR DA GAMA

The king knew it was important to reward the leader of the expedition. First he granted da Gama a yearly pension of 1,000 *cruzados*, a good deal of money at the time. He also gave da Gama the title of "Dom." The title was of great status in the nobility. He also granted him the title of admiral of the seas of India.

Finally, the king granted da Gama what he wanted most. Da Gama asked the king for the lordship of Sines, his birthplace. That meant he would rule over the town and the surrounding lands. King Dom Manuel granted da Gama's wish. He issued a royal edict on December 24, 1499.[5] But, there were problems with this plan.

Sines and the lands around it belonged to the Order of Santiago—a powerful religious group. They would have to agree to give up their hold on the land. The current *alcaidemór* of Sines was a man named D. Luis de Noronha. He needed to be compensated, too. King Dom Manuel wanted to offer other lands in exchange for the title to Sines, but things did not go smoothly. Months went by and an agreement could still not be reached.[6] For the time being, da Gama had to be satisfied with his new wealth and fame.

For the next few years, Vasco da Gama enjoyed his new status. He made one big change in his life:

he married. He wed Dona Catarina de Ataíde. She was the daughter of the late Alvaro de Ataíde. He had been *alcaide*, or governor, of Alvor. Over the years, da Gama and his wife would raise a large family. They had six sons and a daughter.

OTHER VOYAGES TO INDIA

King Dom Manuel was eager to send other voyages to the Far East. He wanted Portugal to rule over parts of India. The Portuguese could then convert the peoples there to Christianity. He also wanted to take part in the rich trade opportunities. He knew Portugal could become even more wealthy and powerful through trade along the Indian coast.

The first expedition King Dom Manuel sent left Lisbon in March 1500. It was a fleet of thirteen ships commanded by Pedro Álvares Cabral. Vasco da Gama helped make all the preparations for this expedition.

In April 1500, Cabral's fleet sighted the coast of Brazil. Cabral claimed the land for Portugal. He sent one ship back to Lisbon to inform the king of his discovery. The trip along the coasts of Africa and around the Cape of Good Hope was difficult. Several ships were lost in severe storms. One of these ships was captained by the famous explorer Bartholmeu Dias. He went down with his vessel.

After several stops along the African coasts, the fleet reached Calicut in September.

The visit to Calicut did not go well. The Zamorin da Gama had visited had died and been replaced by a new, younger man. Cabral and this ruler did not trust each other. On the night of December 16, 1500, nearly eighty Portuguese men who were working ashore in a factory came under attack. More than fifty of the men were killed. The rest barely escaped back to the ships. The attack had come from the Moors, who were still very powerful in Calicut. In revenge, Cabral destroyed ten Arab ships anchored at the docks. He also bombarded the town heavily.[7]

Cabral had better luck in Cochin, India. The ruler there was much more agreeable. Cabral was able to get a rich cargo of spices,

Pedro Álvares Cabral took possession of Brazil for Portugal in April 1500. This nineteenth century engraving shows him holding a sword and raising the Portuguese flag.

porcelain, and cotton. He also left men at Cochin to begin setting up a Portuguese factory. The fleet made one more stop in India, at Cannanur, where they bought more spices.

In late July 1501, Cabral's fleet returned to Portugal. Before Cabral's fleet had returned, King Dom Manuel had sent another voyage to India. This was a small fleet led by João da Nova. They left Portugal in March 1501 and returned eighteen months later. This voyage explored the coast of Brazil and then made many stops along the east coast of Africa. Da Nova's fleet reached India in November 1501. It traveled to Cannanur and Cochin. The fleet was able to take on a good supply of pepper, cinnamon, and sugar before it began its journey home.

Before da Nova even returned home, King Dom Manuel had made a decision. He believed he needed to send a large fleet to establish the Portuguese in India's spice trade. This fleet's main goal would be military action. They would remove the Muslims from their important position in Calicut. This expedition would force the Zamorin there to allow Portugal to participate in the rich spice and gem trade.

This would be a very important voyage. The king knew its success depended on who he chose to lead it. So, again, he turned to Vasco da Gama.

Chapter 6

THE SECOND VOYAGE TO INDIA

Vasco da Gama's second journey to India was much more ambitious than the first. Twenty ships made up the fleet. It would be divided into three squadrons. Da Gama would command the largest one—ten ships. Each of the other two squadrons would be made up of five ships. Da Gama's uncle, Vincente Sodré, would command one squadron. Da Gama's cousin, Estêvão da Gama, would command the other.

As in his first trip to India, Vasco da Gama did not leave his own written record for historians to study. However, there were first-hand accounts of the journey. One record was written by Tomé Lopes. He served as a clerk on one of Estêvão da Gama's ships. The other was written by Mateo de Begnino, another crewmember on one of Estêvão da Gama's vessels.

Vasco da Gama's and Vicente Sodré's squadrons both left Lisbon, Portugal, on February 10, 1502. Estêvão da Gama's squadron sailed on April 1. Together the three squadrons had some eight hundred crewmembers. The ships were also outfitted with large numbers of weapons and artillery. King Dom Manuel was determined to remove the Muslims from their control of the valuable Far East spice trade. He wanted Vasco da Gama to do it by force if necessary.

AROUND THE CAPE AGAIN

The first two squadrons stopped at the Canary Islands and then went to the Cape Verde Islands. There, the ships took on water and wood. By June, the vessels had rounded the Cape of Good Hope. For the rest of that month, da Gama's fleet cruised the southeast coast of Africa. In mid-June they anchored off the port of Sofala. This land was known for its rich trade in gold. Da Gama sent men ashore and established friendly relations with the local ruler. Over the next twelve days, da Gama was able to buy a large amount of gold.

On June 26, the fleet left for Mozambique Island. Two ships that had been separated at the Cape of Good Hope rejoined da Gama's group. At the same time, Vincente Sodré's squadron also rejoined da Gama's main fleet. Da Gama also had a caravel built from extra wood he had brought from Portugal. This caravel, with ten men, would be used for trading along the coast.

On July 12, this combined fleet entered the harbor on the island of Kilwa. It was the most powerful Muslim state on the East African coast. Da Gama knew he would not receive a friendly welcome there. He decided he would impress the Muslims with a Portuguese show of force.

Da Gama's fleet approached Kilwa Kisiwani, the capital—a rich and very populated city. Before they even anchored, da Gama had his ships set off a large round of artillery fire. A short time later, da Gama had a meeting with the Kilwa ruler. His name was Amir Ibrahim. Da Gama demanded that he recognize Portugal's power and submit to its rule. He also demanded that Ibrahim pay a yearly tribute to King Dom Manuel in a large amount of gold. If he did not, da Gama told him, he would burn Kilwa Kisiwani to the ground. Ibrahim had no choice but to agree.

Da Gama was pleased with what he had accomplished. He issued a proclamation in the form of a letter. It described what had happened and what Ibrahim had agreed to. It is one of the very few signed documents by Vasco da Gama that exists.[1]

By July 23, three of Estêvão da Gama's ships had reached Kilwa. The other two ships had been separated in a storm. Together, the combined fleet headed for Malindi. Bad winds caused them to change their course. Instead they headed across the Arabian Sea for India. By August 20, the fleet had reached the island of Anjedive. By early September, the rest of Estêvão da Gama's ships had rejoined the fleet. Da Gama now had his full

On July 12, 1502, da Gama's fleet landed at the harbor of Kilwa Kisiwani (in present-day Tanzania) during his second voyage to India. This photo shows the island today.

number of vessels. He was ready to return to India's coast and carry out his mission.

THE BURNING OF A MUSLIM SHIP

By September, da Gama's fleet was near Cannanur on India's southern coast. Their main goal was to disrupt Muslim shipping. They wanted to capture or destroy these ships and take their cargo.

On September 29, 1502, da Gama's ship the *São Gabriel* came upon a Muslim vessel, the *Mîrî*.

It was returning to Calicut from Mecca. The ship carried more than three hundred people who had gone to Mecca on a pilgrimage. Many wealthy Muslim merchants were on board, and the ship was loaded with riches in spices and gems. Tomé Lopes, a crewmember on board one of da Gama's ships, wrote an account of the event.

Da Gama met with one of the Muslim merchants who owned the ship. The merchant offered to give the admiral several loads of spices if he would let the ship go. Da Gama refused. More negotiations took place. Da Gama took some money and cargo from the vessel.

On October 3, da Gama ordered his men to set fire to the *Mîrî*. What followed was chaos and tragedy. The Muslims onboard knew they were doomed. They tried to get off the vessel. Many women held up their jewelry or their children in an effort to get the Portuguese to rescue them. According to Lopes's account, Vasco da Gama watched all this from his ship and did nothing.

Many people onboard jumped on a Portuguese ship. Hand-to-hand fights broke out. Other Portuguese ships came to the scene. Finally, a Muslim traitor came aboard da Gama's ship. The man told da Gama how to blow up the *Mîrî*. In the words of Tome Lopes, "the Admiral had the said ship burnt with the men who were on it, very cruelly and without any pity."[2]

It is believed that nearly three hundred people died aboard the *Mîrî*. This episode is the most controversial event in Vasco da Gama's career. Some historians claim he showed great cruelty when it was not necessary. He let nearly everyone onboard die when he had already gotten the ship's riches. Others say da Gama was only following King Dom Manuel's orders. He was supposed to destroy the Muslim hold on the Indian spice trade. To do that, he had to put fear into the Muslims. They were the enemy, and he had to show them no mercy.

THE REMAINING MONTHS IN INDIA

Da Gama's fleet spent the next six months along the Indian coast. They stopped at three major ports: Cannanur, Calicut, and Cochin. During this time, da Gama tried to accomplish two major actions at once. He looked for friendly rulers with whom he could make trade deals. He also tried to remove Muslim traders from the control they had over the area.

In each port, da Gama met with some success. But he often had to either threaten the local ruler or use military force to succeed. Of course, on this second voyage, everywhere he went he was in a strong position. He had many ships and many weapons, and did not hesitate to use them.

As in the first voyage, the main problem again turned out to be at Calicut. The fleet anchored there in late October. The Zamorin said he wanted peace with the Portuguese. Da Gama demanded that all Muslims be removed from Calicut. When an agreement could not be reached, da Gama began to bombard the town. Then he captured several ships and seized their cargo. Many people were killed, and much property was destroyed. After several days of this, da Gama left for Cochin. He left Vincente Sodré and six ships behind to blockade Calicut.[3]

Things went better in Cochin. Da Gama had friendly relations with the local ruler. They exchanged gifts. More importantly, there were a number of Portuguese factories operating in Cochin. Because of this, da Gama loaded a large cargo of spices.

Da Gama also met representatives of a Christian order in Cochin. This group numbered about thirty thousand members. Da Gama was pleased to finally have found a group of Christians in a land filled with Muslims and Hindus. In early January, da Gama sent three ships to the port of Kollam. The Christians living there loaded the ships with spices.

While he remained in Cochin, da Gama was visited by three Hindus from Calicut. They carried a letter from the Zamorin. He offered da Gama peace and trade if he would return to Calicut. On January 5, da Gama's fleet left Cochin.

Things went bad in Calicut. Shortly after their arrival, da Gama's fleet was attacked in the middle of the night. The attackers came in nearly eighty small boats. The men climbed aboard da Gama's ships and his men had to fight them off in hand-to-hand combat. Then, Vincente Sodré's ships joined the battle. They drove off the attackers and killed many of them.

Da Gama vowed revenge. He hanged three Indians and paraded them on his ship before the

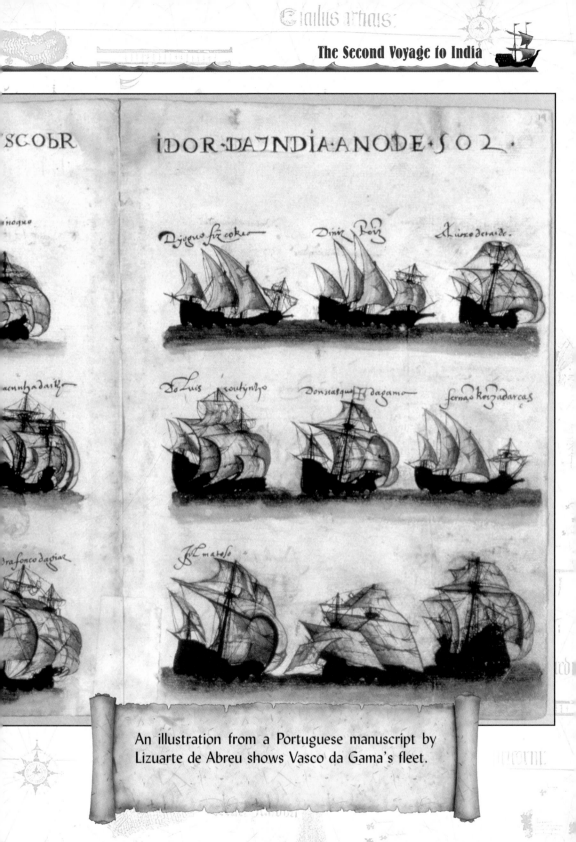

An illustration from a Portuguese manuscript by Lizuarte de Abreu shows Vasco da Gama's fleet.

whole town. Then da Gama's fleet left to make stops at Cannanur and Cochin. They intended to finish loading spices and get ready for the return voyage home to Portugal. Then da Gama learned the Calicut Zamorin had gathered a very large fleet to attack the Portuguese ships.

The Zamorin had put together a fleet of more than thirty large ships and many smaller vessels. The total number of men was probably about 7,000. Most of the men were from the *Mappila* community.

The attack took place as da Gama's vessels were back in the waters off Calicut. Da Gama used a heavy bombardment against the Muslim ships. The Muslims suffered great casualties. Many of them jumped overboard to escape the bombardment and drowned. Two enemy ships were captured and burned as the Zamorin watched helplessly from his palace ashore.[4] The Portuguese had won an important victory.

Da Gama sailed for Cannanur. Word had already reached there of his success against the *Mappilas*. Da Gama entered in a new agreement of friendship with Cannanur's ruler. They added Cochin to the deal and it became a three-way alliance against the Zamorin of Calicut.

Da Gama was ready to return to Portugal. Before he left Cannanur, he set up a permanent Portuguese factory there with twenty men. He also left five ships behind under Vincente Sodré's command. They would continue to interfere with Muslim shipping and trade in the nearby areas. On February 20, 1503, da Gama's thirteen-ship fleet sailed for home.

GOING HOME

The trip home lasted eight months. By mid-April, the fleet had reached Mozambique. The vessels were repaired and stocked with fresh supplies. Da Gama sent the ships back in groups of two and three. The first two ships reached Lisbon by the end of August. Da Gama left southeast Africa in late June. He arrived in Lisbon on October 10, 1503, aboard the *São Jeronimo*. By the end of October, all thirteen ships had made it safely home. The fleet had returned with almost two thousand tons of spices, most of it pepper.

Da Gama's second voyage to India was an even greater success than the first. The huge cargo of spices would be worth a great deal of money. He had formed an alliance with the rulers of two key Indian trade cities. He had defeated the Zamorin of Calicut in a decisive battle. Portugal was now established as an important trading partner in India. Just as importantly, it was also a country to be feared and respected—in Europe and Asia.

Chapter 7

YEARS OF FORTUNE AND INFLUENCE

Soon after his return, Vasco da Gama had an audience with King Dom Manuel. Once again, the king praised da Gama for his great success in India. In return, da Gama presented the king with a large silver basin. In it were the five hundred gold coins that da Gama had demanded in tribute from the sultan of Kilwa. From this gold, the king had a gold tabernacle cast and presented it to the church at Belem.

For the next twenty years, da Gama assumed the life of a Portuguese citizen. He would spend his time living in Lisbon and elsewhere. As with his early life, there are not many details known about how da Gama spent these years.

During this time, da Gama and his wife began to raise a family. They would eventually have seven children. Sometime between 1504 and 1506, da Gama moved his family back to his hometown of Sines. His goal was to build a large manor house as well as other buildings. He also wanted to assume the title of lordship of Sines. This was the title that King Dom Manuel had granted him in 1499. However, for

After King Dom Manuel ordered Vasco da Gama to leave Sines, he moved his family to Évora where he lived for several years. This photo shows the Cathedral of Évora (at top) and the Portas de Moura Square.

different reasons, da Gama had never been able to claim it.

Now there was still a problem. The town was under the rule of the religious group the Order of Santiago. King Dom Manuel's nephew, Dom Jorge, was the leader of this group. He refused to give up his role and protested to the king. The king sided

with his nephew. He told da Gama to stop building his new house and the other buildings. He also ordered da Gama and his family to leave Sines and not to return unless Dom Jorge granted his permission. Da Gama gave in to the king's order. He moved his family to Évora, where they would live for the next several years.[1]

THE GROWING PORTUGUESE EMPIRE IN INDIA

Over the next several years, Portugal strengthened its growing empire in India. Other voyages were sent in 1504 and 1505. The Portuguese established outposts in places such as Cochin and Cannanur. They also set up forts along the East African coast.

In 1505, King Dom Manuel appointed a viceroy for Portugal's Asian outposts. This person would govern and organize Portuguese possessions in India. King Dom Manuel picked Dom Francisco de Almeida, a powerful nobleman, for the job. De Almeida sailed to India with a fleet of twenty-two ships and more than 2,500 men. Half the ships were to return to Portugal filled with cargo. The rest of the fleet would remain behind to protect Portugal's settlements.

De Almeida held the position for the next four years. During that time, Portugal continued to strengthen its position in the Far East. Numerous voyages went back and forth carrying large cargoes of spices. The Muslims began to lose their control of the Indian and Far Eastern trade they had held for many years.

De Almeida governed until 1509. Then he was replaced by Alfonso de Albuquerque. During his rule, Portugal began to control other important trade centers. De Albuquerque captured Hormuz at the mouth of the Persian Gulf. In 1510, he took the important Muslim port of Goa along the Indian coast. Goa would be the Portuguese capital in India for the next four hundred years. Alfonso de Albuquerque served until his death in 1515. By then Portugal's role in the Far East trade was firmly in place.

A Title for Da Gama

During these years, Vasco da Gama lived well. He received revenues from Sines and the surrounding towns. He was allowed to import products from India without having to pay the duty and freight charges. In 1515, King Dom Manuel granted him a yearly pension of 60,000 *reais*. This money was for his office of Admiral of the Indian Sea.

In 1518, da Gama asked King Dom Manuel to grant him the title of count. Da Gama said the king had promised him this title. It was to be a reward for his long service to the Crown. Da Gama told the king he would ask permission to leave Portugal if the title was not granted.

This was no small matter. The title of count would raise da Gama's family to the high noble ranks. King Dom Manuel waited several months, but he finally rewarded da Gama. He did not want to let da Gama leave his kingdom. In December 1519, da Gama became the Count of Vidigueira.[2]

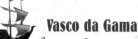

Alfonso de Albuquerque served as viceroy for Portugal's outposts in India and Asia from 1509 until his death in 1515.

It was a town located in Alentejo, the region where da Gama was born.

Da Gama moved his family there in 1520. They were well received by the local people. The family moved into the town's castle and it became their permanent residence. Da Gama remained there for the next four years. He managed his property and paid for improvements in the town. He led the life of a retired noble. In 1524, things changed. Once again, his country called on him for a very important job.

SERVING A NEW KING

In December 1521, King Dom Manuel died. His eldest son, who was nineteen years old, succeeded him. He became King João III. The new king worried about Portugal's possessions in India. There had been problems in recent years. Things were not well organized in many ports. Some officials were only interested in taking money or goods for themselves.

By 1523, the king decided he needed to put a new person in charge. He needed a strong person with experience. He wanted someone who knew India well, and he wanted someone who would protect the interests of the Crown—by brute force if necessary. So, in January 1524, the king named Vasco da Gama the new viceroy of Portuguese India. He would make one more voyage to the place of his greatest triumphs.

Chapter 8

Return to India and Glory

On April 9, 1524, Vasco da Gama set sail for India. His fleet this time was the grandest he ever had. Fourteen ships, including seven large vessels, made up the fleet. The men aboard numbered about three thousand. Many of them had served in the king's court. They were of good background and good education. Two of da Gama's sons, Estêvão and Paulo, were also on the voyage. Estêvão was a ship's captain and had the title of captain-major of the Indian seas.[1]

Da Gama's fleet also carried a new group of government officials. These officials would replace the men in several Portuguese forts in India and elsewhere. There would be new captains for forts in Hormuz, Goa, Cannanur, and Cochin. It was part of the king's plan to give Portuguese India a stronger and more honest government.

The fleet had a fairly smooth trip around the Cape of Good Hope. It reached Mozambique on August 15. They added supplies and made repairs. Da Gama also sent a letter and gifts to the king of Malindi. In the past, he had been very friendly to the Portuguese. Da Gama apologized for not visiting him on this voyage. He was in a great hurry to reach India.

The crossing of the Indian Ocean was rough. Four vessels were lost. Then in early September, the fleet was off the Indian coast near Dabul. Suddenly, the sea trembled violently. The men became very frightened. They were ready to abandon the ships. Da Gama knew what was happening. He stood on deck and calmed the men. "Do not be afraid," he told them. "This is an earthquake."[2] Soon, the danger passed. Once again, da Gama had shown courage in a crisis.

A few days later, the fleet met up with a Muslim ship returning to India loaded with gold coins and valuable cargo. Da Gama captured the vessel, seizing the money and goods. There was no repeat of what happened with the *Mîrî*. This time da Gama did not destroy the vessel or harm the crew.[3] On September 15, the fleet anchored at the port of Chaul. For the first time in more than twenty years, Vasco da Gama was back in India.

THE VICEROY TAKES COMMAND

As soon as they reached India, da Gama took on his new title of viceroy. He quickly went to work. He began to replace the local Portuguese officials. Many of these officials were either dishonest or incompetent. Da Gama gave their jobs to men he had brought with him from Portugal. Many of these men were members of the nobility and they would be loyal to the king.

The fleet departed Chaul, and on September 23, they anchored near Goa. Da Gama received a grand welcome in Goa. Members of the local Portuguese council were very pleased to see him. They even offered him gifts, which he refused. Da Gama quickly replaced Goa's captain of the fort, Francisco Pereira Pestana. The Portuguese settlers in Goa believed Pestana was dishonest, but they could not get rid of him. He was a close ally of the governor, Dom Duarte de Meneses.

Da Gama named a trusted noble, Dom Henrique de Meneses (of no relation to the governor), to replace Pestana. Da Gama took other actions while in Goa. He issued an order that anyone sailing the Indian Ocean had to have a license. Anyone who owned a ship had to sign a contract with a Portuguese official. Otherwise the ship would be seized and the cargo taken. He also ordered that anyone found to have taken property of the Crown would be sent back to Portugal for good.[4]

Da Gama remained in Goa for nearly a month. The fleet then sailed for Cochin. On the way, they met up with a fleet commanded by Dom Luis de Meneses. He was the brother of the present governor. He was on his way to meet his brother's fleet in Hormuz. Instead, da Gama ordered de Meneses to follow him to Cochin.

Vasco da Gama's explorations inspired other explorers and mapmakers. The Miller Atlas was produced around 1519 and shows the Indian Ocean, the Persian Gulf, India, and North Africa.

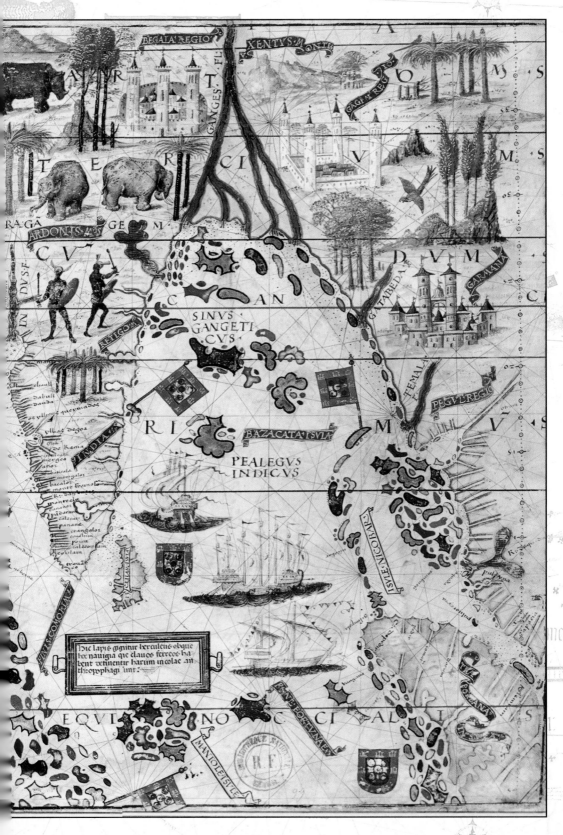

BEGALA REGIO

XENTYS MONTE

GAGE REG.

AR T

GANGES FL.

CI V

TER RI

RAGĀ

ARDONIS ABS GE M

CV

DUM

GATABEDA

GARMANA

C A N

C

SINVS
GANGETI
CVS

REIIGO

RI

BAZACATA ISVLA

M

PEGVL REGIO

EMALA

V AS

INDIA

PEALEGVS
INDICVS

ISVLE NICOBAR

ANTROCOMORUM

Hic lapis gignitur berculeus obque
hoc naugia qie claues ferreos ha
bent veninentur harum incolae an
thropophagi unt.

EQVI

NO

CCI AL I

S

NANIOLE ISVLE

The two fleets made a brief stop in Cannanur. As in Chaul and Goa, da Gama also replaced the fort's captain there. Then the fleets left for Cochin. In late October 1524, da Gama still had much he wanted to accomplish, but he did not know then that he was quickly running out of time.

THE FINAL MONTHS

They arrived in Cochin in early November. Vasco da Gama appointed a new captain of the fort, Dom Lope Vaz de Sampaio. He also appointed Afonso Meixa as the new comptroller of revenue. This job was the head of finance for all of Portuguese India. It was a powerful job, second in command to the viceroy. With that done, da Gama took steps to remove the present governor from his position.

Governor Dom Duarte de Meneses arrived back in Cochin in early December. Da Gama would not let him come ashore. Instead, he sent a committee headed by de Sampaio and Meixa to

Da Gama visited Goa for nearly a month during his final voyage to India. Above, is the Viceroy's Arch in Old Goa.

meet with him. They gave the governor two letters. One letter came directly from King João III. The letter ordered him to hand over his command to Vasco da Gama. It also ordered him to return to Portugal as soon as possible.[5]

The other letter was from da Gama. It ordered the governor to return to Portugal aboard the ship *Castello*. He was to remain on board as a prisoner and not go ashore until he reached Lisbon. The governor's brother, Dom Luis, tried to speak up for him. He told da Gama that his brother might have his faults, but "at least he never sold one of the King's fortresses." Da Gama then replied, "Sir, if your brother had sold fortresses, he would not have his head where it is now, for I should have ordered it to be cut off."[6]

De Meneses at first refused to leave his own ship, the *São Jorge*. Da Gama then threatened to use artillery against him. Finally, de Meneses gave in. He agreed to the transfer of power. He moved to the ship *Castello* and prepared to leave India.

Since his return to India, da Gama had been quite busy. It had been a very stressful time and he was not well. In fact, by mid-December it was clear to others that he had become very ill. Da Gama knew this himself. He soon made plans for others to carry on his work.

Chapter 9

A Lasting Impact on History

By mid-December, da Gama moved his living quarters from the fortress at Cochin to the house of Diogo Pereira. He was an elderly man who lived near the church courtyard. Da Gama knew he was dying, so he began to put his affairs in order.

His first concern was about who would succeed him. He worried that Duarte de Meneses would try to reclaim his position as governor. De Meneses had still not left for Portugal. So, da Gama had papers drawn up, sworn to, and signed by his top aide, Afonso Meixa. These papers said that if da Gama died, Dom Lope Vaz de Sampaio would serve as a temporary governor. Da Gama had already named de Sampaio the captain of the fort at Cochin. The name of a permanent successor would be revealed later. These papers also set down regulations to be followed until the new governor took over.

Da Gama then put his personal life in order. He had already taken care of his affairs at home. His oldest son, Dom Francisco, would receive his titles and estates when he died. His sons, Estêvão and Paulo, were in India with him. They were to dispose of his personal effects.

He wanted his clothes and furniture to be donated to churches and hospitals. He asked his sons to return to Portugal following his death.

Da Gama died on Christmas Eve, December 24, 1524. His return to India had lasted only three months. He died thousands of miles away from home. Yet, he died in the place that would be connected to his name throughout history.

The tomb of Vasco da Gama at the Jeronimoes monastery in Lisbon, Portugal. He died on Christmas Eve, December 24, 1524.

Vasco da Gama was buried in the chapel of the Portuguese church of Santo Antonio in Cochin. The ceremony was marked with full honors for a man who had reached such noble and military status. Shortly after the funeral, the leading nobles in Cochin came together. They opened the royal letters of succession signed by the king. The letters revealed da Gama's permanent successor as governor—Dom Henrique de Meneses. Da Gama had named him as the new captain of the fort in Goa back in September. Now, he would be the leader of all of Portuguese India.[1]

Vasco da Gama's final request was to eventually have his body brought back home. In 1538, his son Dom Pedro de Silva Gama took the remains from Cochin back to Portugal. They were buried in a church in Vidigueira. The family estates were still there. More than three hundred years later the remains were moved again. In 1898, they were reburied in the monastery of Jeronimoes at Belém. They were placed next to the remains of Portugal's famous literary figure, the poet Luíz Vaz de Camões. This was a resting place of national honor.

THE LEGACY OF VASCO DA GAMA

It is not always easy to judge a person's impact on world history. One way is to see how much that

The Vasco da Gama Bridge in Lisbon, Portugal.

person helped change the world during his or her lifetime.

When Vasco da Gama was born in 1469, Portugal was a small European country. It had few natural resources. Its sources of wealth were not great. By the time he died in 1524, Portugal's status in Europe had greatly changed. Portugal had become a leading power. Its empire reached from around the coasts of Africa to the Persian Gulf, India, and Asia. Through its trading networks, it had obtained great wealth. It was also a feared

military and naval power, both in Europe and around the globe.

Vasco da Gama played a key role in these changes. His first historic voyage to India paved the way for Portugal's and Europe's entry into trade in Asia. His second expedition showed how the Portuguese military could be successful against a larger number of hostile forces. His final voyage helped begin a period of reform for Portugal's empire. It would allow that empire to last for hundreds of years.

During his lifetime, da Gama also gained great wealth and status. He was awarded titles and large land holdings. After his death, his heirs enjoyed the same status for hundreds of years.

Of course, his life was not without controversy. His behavior at times was cruel and ruthless. Like other European explorers, he sometimes mistreated peoples in the foreign lands he visited. He showed no mercy to his enemies. His defenders claim his good deeds and important achievements far outweigh his failings. In Portugal, he has been a national hero for centuries. The world has looked upon Vasco da Gama as one of the great explorers in history.

Chapter Notes

Chapter 1. A Great Sea Voyage Ends in Glory

1. Henry H. Hart, *Sea Road to the Indies* (New York: The MacMillan Company, 1950), p. 156.

2. K. D. Madan, *Life and Travels of Vasco da Gama* (New Delhi, India: Asian Educational Services, 1998), pp. xxvii–xxviii.

Chapter 2. Early Life of an Explorer

1. Sanjay Subrahmanyam, *The Career and Legend of Vasco da Gama* (Cambridge: Cambridge University Press, 1997), pp. 61–62.

2. Ronald Watkins, *Unknown Seas* (London: John Murray Publishers, 2003), p. 149.

3. K. G. Jayne, *Vasco da Gama and His Successors 1460–1580* (New York: Barnes and Noble, Inc., 1970), p. 27.

4. Watkins, p. 116.

5. Ibid., p. 118.

6. Subrahmanyam, p. 63.

7. Watkins, p. 146.

8. Subrahmanyam, pp. 67–68.

9. Watkins, pp. 155–156.

10. K. D. Madan, *Life and Travels of Vasco da Gama* (New Delhi, India: Asian Educational Services, 1998), pp. 29–30.

11. Watkins, p. 158–159.

12. Jayne, p. 37.

Chapter 3. Sailing the Coasts of Africa

1. Ronald Watkins, *Unknown Seas* (London: John Murray Publishers, 2003), p. 177.

2. *Roteiro, A Journal of the First Voyage of Vasco da Gama*, 1497–1499, trans. and ed. E. G. Ravenstein, (Hakluyt Society, 1898), p. 8

3. Sanjay Subrahmanyam, *The Career and Legend of Vasco da Gama* (Cambridge: Cambridge University Press, 1997), pp. 87–88.

4. *Roteiro*, p. 13.

5. Ibid., pp. 20–21.

6. Subrahmanyam, p. 118.

7. *Roteiro*, pp. 37–38.

8. Ibid., pp. 45–46

Chapter 4. India and the Journey Home

1. Sanjay Subrahmanyam, *The Career and Legend of Vasco da Gama* (Cambridge: Cambridge University Press, 1997), p. 103.

2. K. D. Madan, *Life and Travels of Vasco da Gama* (New Delhi, India: Asian Educational Services, 1998), p. 44.

3. *Roteiro, A Journal of the First Voyage of Vasco da Gama*, 1497–1499, trans. and ed. E.G. Ravenstein, (Hakluyt Society, 1898), pp. 49–50.

4. Ronald Watkins, *Unknown Seas* (London: John Murray Publishers, 2003), pp. 260–261.

5. Ibid., p. 265.

6. *Roteiro*, p. 77.

Chapter 5. A Hero to His Country

1. Ronald Watkins, *Unknown Seas* (London: John Murray Publishers, 2003), pp. 288–289.

2. Sanjay Subrahmanyam, *The Career and Legend of Vasco da Gama* (Cambridge: Cambridge University Press, 1997), p. 159

3. Watkins, pp. 289–290.

4. Glenn J. Ames, *Vasco da Gama: Renaissance Crusader* (New York: Pearson Education, Inc., 2005), pp. 73–75.

5. Subrahmanyam, p. 167.

6. Ibid., pp. 167–168.

7. K. D. Madan, *Life and Travels of Vasco da Gama* (New Delhi, India: Asian Educational Services, 1998), p. 71.

Chapter 6. The Second Voyage to India
1. Sanjay Subrahmanyam, *The Career and Legend of Vasco da Gama* (Cambridge: Cambridge University Press, 1997), p. 202.
2. Ibid., pp. 205–206.
3. K. D. Madan, *Life and Travels of Vasco da Gama* (New Delhi, India: Asian Educational Services, 1998), pp. 85–86.
4. Subrahmanyam, pp. 222–223.

Chapter 7. Years of Fortune and Influence
1. Sanjay Subrahmanyam, *The Career and Legend of Vasco da Gama* (Cambridge: Cambridge University Press, 1997), pp. 242–244.
2. Ibid., p. 281.

Chapter 8. Return to India and Glory
1. Sanjay Subrahmanyam, *The Career and Legend of Vasco da Gama* (Cambridge: Cambridge University Press, 1997), pp. 305–306.
2. K. G. Jayne, *Vasco da Gama and His Successors 1460–1580* (New York: Barnes and Noble, Inc., 1970), p. 124.
3. K. D. Madan, *Life and Travels of Vasco da Gama* (New Delhi, India: Asian Educational Services, 1998), p. 118.
4. Ibid., pp. 120–121.
5. Subrahmanyam, p. 333.
6. Jayne, p. 127.

Chapter 9. A Lasting Impact on History
1. K. D. Madan, *Life and Travels of Vasco da Gama* (New Delhi, India: Asian Educational Services, 1998), p. 126

Glossary

alliance—An agreement between individuals or nations to form an association to further common interests.

astrolabe—An instrument used to observe and determine the position of heavenly bodies, such as the sun, the moon, and the stars.

astronomy—The study of objects and matter outside the earth's atmosphere.

boatswain—A petty officer on a merchant vessel.

bow—The front end of a boat.

caravel—A small sailing ship used during the 15th and 16th centuries

cruzados—Portuguese gold coins.

expedition—A journey taken for a specific reason.

flagship—The ship that carries the commander of a fleet and flies his flag.

Hindu—A person who follows Hinduism, the major religion of India.

interpreter—A person who explains the meanings of words to speakers of different languages.

mast—A long pole on the deck of a ship that supports other ship parts, such as sails.

Moors—A tribe of Arab peoples originally from northern Africa.

Muslim—A person who follows the religion of Islam.

nautical—Having to do with seamen, navigation, or ships. A nautical mile is equal to approximately 6,076 feet.

navigation—The act or study of getting ships, aircraft, or spacecraft from place to place.

noble—A person of high rank or birth.

padrão—A stone column inscribed with the royal crest of Portugal.

pardon—An order that excuses a crime or an offense with no further punishment.

pilgrimage—A journey made to a shrine or a holy place.

recruit—To hire or sign up new members for a group or an assignment.

retainer—A person owing service to a household, such as a servant.

scurvy—A disease marked by very soft gums, loose teeth, and bleeding into the skin, caused by a lack of vitamin C.

squadron—A naval unit made up of two or more divisions and, sometimes, additional vessels.

stern—The rear end of a boat.

tributary—A stream feeding a larger stream, river, or lake.

tribute—A payment by one ruler or nation to another as a way of honoring or submitting to them.

viceroy—The governor of a country or province who rules as a representative of a king.

Further Reading

Books

Bailey, Katharine. *Vasco da Gama: Quest for the Spice Trade*. New York: Crabtree Publishing, 2007.

Calvert, Patricia. *Vasco da Gama: So Strong a Spirit*. New York: Benchmark Books, 2005.

Draper, Allison Stark. *Vasco Da Gama: The Portuguese Quest for a Sea Route from Europe to India*. New York: Rosen, 2005.

Gritzner, Charles F. and Douglas A. Phillips. *Portugal*. New York: Chelsea House Publishers, 2007.

Koestler-Grack, Rachel. *Vasco da Gama and the Sea Route to India*. New York: Chelsea House Publications, 2005.

Internet Addresses

The European Voyages of Exploration:
The Sea-Route to India and Vasco da Gama
<http://www.ucalgary.ca/applied_history/tutor/eurvoya/vasco.html>

The Mariners' Museum—Age of Exploration:
Portuguese Explorers
<http://www.mariner.org/education/portuguese-explorers>

Modern History Sourcebook:
Vasco da Gama
<http://www.fordham.edu/halsall/mod/1497degama.html>